THE CALLING BOOKS

THE SOUL'S JOURNEY TO LOVE

Valentina M. Grosvenor

Copyright © 2024 by Valentina M. Grosvenor

All rights reserved.

No portion of this book may be reproduced in any form without written permission from the author, except as permitted by Canada and U.S. copyright law. For permission requests, contact: info@thecallingbooks.com

Book cover by Valentina M. Grosvenor

First Edition, 2024

DISCLAIMER

The information within this book is given in good faith, received from a source outside of the author, and is considered spiritual advice relating to life's issues. It is not intended to diagnose any physical or mental condition nor to serve as a substitute for informed medical advice or care. Please contact a competent health professional if assistance or counseling is needed. If you are experiencing urgent spiritual issues and distress, consult a practitioner with an awareness and competency in spiritual emergence and spiritual emergencies.

The author cannot be held liable by any person for any loss or damage whatsoever which may arise from the use of this book or any of the information therein.

Contents

Dear Humanity,

Let there be light upon the Soul.

Acknowledgements

Thank you Source, God, the All That Is, for the words that flowed, your wisdom, truth, and the gifts you have bestowed in me.

To my spiritual family for healing, teaching, and grounding me and my gifts in this physical world.

To my spirit guides, angels, and ancestors for guiding me each day. Your presence is a gift.

Finally, to my family and friends for surrounding me with love and believing in me through my hardest times.

Preface
by Valentina M Grosvenor

In each individual soul there exists a burning need to be seen, to be known, to show ourselves as the being that we are. A being of light. Suppressed through the lives and living within a structured society, we begin to dim ourselves based on how others have reacted, how we have experienced times where we have dared to put our full selves forward. We diminish, yet often we do not even know from where or when this has occurred. We come to a point in our lives where we see that something is amiss. A feeling. A knowing.

This transcription is part of my knowing. It began as an inquiry into my own soul at a time when career and family life were at its highest. Yet something wasn't quite right. I could not place my finger on it; elusive, wanting to set fire to me but not sure how. I was not a spiritual being at this point in time. To be spiritual meant you attend church, ceremonies and the like; an action that I could not see the value of in my day-to-day life. As I progressed down the line of inquiry, the simple act of meditation created the space for me to ceremony, with myself. And with this inward focus, sitting with my own soul, a familiar and renowned Elder came to assist me. My first in a long series of guides that would come along my way. He came as a strong and steady figure to root me in my own knowing. Knowing that he was with me, from the other side, gave me strength to keep going, keep listening, keep believing.

When we come upon that place in time when we ask ourselves "what is it that I must do," we awaken a world of gifts within us that have been burning to come out to the light. They were buried at some point—many feel they had them all along yet I still cannot seem to find the time when I originally saw, felt and heard what I do now. The gifts come as a reminder of our power, the skill that we inherently all have, the skills that we have pushed aside for the dogma of society have told us it is simply imagination. But what if that gift is trying to tell us something? What if we are meant to be here to exert our influence through our God-given gifts for a greater purpose than we could ever imagine? Carry on reading, you shall see why.

The words that follow are a signal to all, that when we allow our power to be seen by our selves we can generate marvels upon marvels of experiences, knowledge, wisdom, when we let it flow. For me, the words were simply journal writings to start. My words flowed effortlessly as if they were already at the tip of my pen waiting to be written. Thoughts transferred immediately to the page, sometimes as my thoughts, and other times disparate in the form of intuition, inner voice or higher self.

And then began the words from somewhere else, not my own. I was instructed by the voice: *"Write this down."* I put what I was doing aside and sat to write. And once finished, *"The End."* It was clear, it was profound, it was not mine. It was relevant to me in what I was going through, but it also had much wiser and broader implications and application. I wrote frequently—my experiences, my dreams, the wisdom—in order to make sense of what did not at the time. A knowing that maybe one day it would. The words were profound, nothing which I could imagine or dream up much less transcribe to paper without one correction or thought to reframe. It came. And it came.

As I enquired through spiritual and metaphysical texts and teachers about the various experiences I was encountering on my journey I came to realize (and accept) that I, a modern-day woman, mother, and professional working and living a very typical life, was a conscious channeler. A bridge between physical and spiritual realms. In all cases when receiving this information I was conscious and aware of the process but not in control of the information that was being relayed. There was a unique tone, patter, and loving, benevolent nature to the transmission. And so I allowed and trusted in something I could not see but could feel and know deeply to be true.

Channeling is a form of communicating with, or receiving communication from, higher beings or consciousness and can occur naturally or during deep trance states. The person receiving information is often referred to as a vessel, container or vehicle through which messages are transmitted to, and information can come through automatic writing, or through voice.

Automatic writing, or psychography, involves writing without conscious thought. In a relaxed, trance-like state, words are allowed to flow onto paper without actively thinking about them.

With these two skills now taking a very present function in my life as I document and navigate my awakening spirit, I was not yet aware that these skills were paving the way to something much bigger than I could ever anticipate. The instructions, words, and guidance were bigger than me and my lonely individual journey. It was the making of words that are meant for the world to see and hear, benevolent, and cherishing of every one of our journeys. Together.

On November 6th, 2022 it became clear. My first book—*The Soul's Journey to Love.* It would take additional sessions sitting with this profound source of wisdom to learn that this was to be the first in a series of five books intended to assist people on their journeys of awakening and serving to provide clarity in why this awakening matters so much. To ourselves, to each other, to humanity as a whole. Ultimately, our lives depend on it. Our happiness depends on it.

I welcome you to read this with an open heart and open mind. Other sources of similar information exist, and I do not propose that this transmission is the sole source of truth and guidance. Transmissions are occurring through many vessels in order to reach humanity in the various stages each individual may be, and with information that is pertinent and relevant to them. References to God are meant to be all-encompassing of the higher power that various religions and cultures acknowledge to exist and having their own naming convention. Other terms—Source, Truth, Creator, or the All That Is—are as transcribed.

As clear as the instructions were to write, the time to publish was made equally clear. With this first book, my soul burns bright once again with the knowing of what it is capable of. Let this knowing help you along the way, giving you the wisdom and faith to keep going until you have achieved all that you are meant to.

May I be of service. May I be the channel that guides people home. To themselves.

Introduction

This book is the first in a series of channeled wisdom brought down from Source Consciousness through the well-known art of wisdom-keeper—a person who has been given authority to transcribe the word of God based on their history as a soul charged with responsibility to hear, see, and speak the truth of all known wisdom in the spiritual realms. The wisdom-keeper is gifted with senses that when transmuted to humanly words has the power to transmit energy from the Divine, God, Source, Gaia, or however one wishes to refer to the spirit of oneness. These words are guided through the wisdom-keeper to transform the seeker into one who sees their own light.

The magical powers within us are meant to be found and fostered. Through spiritual seeking one comes to hold the words that are meant for them and in a way that brings power to their life force again. The wisdom held in these books will find their way to the hearts of those who are ready to change the world. One soul at a time.

The author chooses to remain anonymous out of respect for the wisdom that is not theirs and in keeping with the Laws of Relativity. That which we reap we sow. Fostering a greater sense of trust in the unknown is necessary on the individual and the collective level by way of releasing the power and identification that comes from authorship. Here, a place of complete surrender into the unknown occurs whilst the words filter throughout the world.

The author's experiences in ascension have no doubt played a role in this message, but rather than influence the message based upon personal reflection and subjective interpretation of these experiences, the words here are pure Source achieved through the meticulous care and protection of the vessel that which is the authors. It is of paramount importance the continued protection of this vessel for the words of Source to continue manifesting through earth.

Let there be light, let there be fame through the collective benefits of this transmission.

Chapter 1
By the Light We See

There was a chill in the night air, a stillness that could only be broken with the edge of a knife. An awkward stillness that could only mean impending doom. It was history that would repeat itself centuries after centuries. A dislike for calm and happiness. For what good would that be for.

There is a drama that ensues when the world is in chaos, a low hum amongst people, an unsatisfaction with all that is. A hunger, a yearning for more and more. A thirst that cannot be quenched. A conspiracy amongst those who want to have it all, the power, the glory, the righteousness. And in that righteousness is a bleeding through of emotions that never get to see the light of day. And so, they fester. Simmering beneath the wounds, calluses that grow even harder, thicker as the time goes on. Pinching the wound would make it spread, and so, rather than releasing the pressure it grows internally. Within the bones, the sheathing of the muscles, tendons. It acts like a glue that is desperate to stay in place, tentacles reaching as far as the depths allow. Every part of every body can become consumed by this pain before turning into sickness. For one cannot bear this pain without an effect on some distal part of the psyche or the soul.

Interwoven are the human processes, delicately intertwined to bring our worldly existence into reality. A reality that is chosen by us but perpetuated by the souls around us who have equally lost their way. At the heart of our being is to reach transcendence, of not only our shadows but the shadows of others. A coming home to peace and calm, despite the chaos and despite the pain we bring forth to ourselves and to others. For there will be no more pain when the chaos stops. And so, you shall ask, how does one or many move out from the chaos? How does chaos stop when it feeds our desires of the lower realm—greed, power, money? How does one turn their back to the life it only knows and move towards peace and calm?

It lays within. Let me tell you how.

From the moment we are conceived, your life force only serves you for your highest good, for nourishment, warmth, the gentle sounds of a mother's voice, the soothing motion as she walks through life. The stillness as she sleeps is when you are reaching for her, the turning, the brushing, to make yourself known. From this point on, you are seeking love and affection from something outside of you. The stimulation from the outer world that can be felt the moment you have skin, eyes, and ears. The sensations are gentle yet present, a reminder that you are carried, supported in a womb of love, strength, and devotion that will carry you through to your first breath.

Allowing, trusting, that all is well.

There is nothing you need to do. There is nothing you need to do but let Gaia, your mother, walk you into the earthly world.

There is a flow to this allowing that brings a notable peace to a mother. A calm, centered place at her belly where growth can take place. Only in the woman's womb can such creation take place, for it is here where the new world meets the old. And it is here that fear and trauma can either be magnified throughout history or be transmuted and be gone forever.

The heart beating signifies the strength of love for Gaia and other earthly beings, whether plant, animal, or human. The valves and chambers functioning in unison, without regard to the external. It plays the eternal role of physical life. Pumping the purity of life-giving force through every part of the body, providing nourishment and water at all times. It is here that the nervous system connects to the functions of our mind and of our soul. The mind is one of introspective and retrospective vision, so to speak, that captures all information relating to the body—sensations, stimulations—and turning them into memories. It is here wherein lay the key to removing pain and trauma. To turn those stimulants into powers to change chaos to peace, trauma to stillness.

As the story unfolds, become aware of the shifts in your perception, your perspective and the stillness you feel in your core. Become one with the words as they cross your mind, undoing, unfolding, untangling the chaos you have become to know and live within. Become aware of a new way of seeing and feeling.

Chapter 2
The Dawn of a New Day

An era of scorn and greed is unfolding, bleeding through the pores of those tortured by prior generations. Their sins carry on for generations in the hopes that they will soon see the error of their ways. The sickness carried in the hearts who have come before us, tainted by choices that only can harm. The Choice. This is one's turning point. To harm or not to harm. To forgive or to not forgive. To love and devotion, or scorn and faithlessness.

To choose the side of love carries enormous power to heal and return the pain felt before us to Source where it can one day be brought into the energetic realms of love. Pain is purified through choosing love. Not just any love. A soul love that shatters boundaries. Not the fleeting love of lust or passion. The soul knows this love when it sees it. Time nor space can bring this love apart.

It is the soul's search for this love that sets it apart from others. The unshakable feeling, the glimpses of future times, and the pain of past attempts. There is no coming back from the search unscathed for it will enter every part of your living and breathing space, making itself known to you, not to be forgotten until the search is over. To be feeling the depths of your soul apart is the beginning of the strength that will lead you to one another. The wonder of it all, is what binds you, clearing the path one stone at a time, one event at a time, one breath at a time. This is the power that is beholden upon true soul love. Thou shalt not falter, thou shalt not fail on this journey. There is only one outcome, only one place.

The union of soul love brings heaven to earth, a commonly misinterpreted symbol of reaching ecstasy. In the state of union, a new embodiment of love is found, a repairing of gridlines that ripple through the matrix. A wave of healing trauma lines and trauma bonds. This love is the highest. It is the most sought after, yet most difficult to find when buried beneath the sea of doing and forcing, rather than being and creating. It is not possible to create from within the storm. It is on the outside, in the calm, where soul finds you and your rightful purpose. In the subtle waves in stillness that can only be felt once truly connected to your soul. Waves of resonance filling your mind space, your heart space, and your womb space.

The creation story begins by telling us of two beautiful souls, Adam and Eve, surrounded by abundance, beauty, life, and peacefulness. In harmonious love, the story would not have turned into the concept that it is, of temptation, of indulgence. The story unfolded as it should with only our minds capable of distorting what only two people would have in their own hearts known. **The presumption that others around us know better is a fallacy born from our fear of our own choices, and the greed of**

others who seek power over you. Left to their own choices they would not have failed.

There is a power in choosing for one's own purpose and highest good. This power cannot be mistaken for selfishness and greed, for it is an all-encompassing power, not one of exclusion and righteousness. It is harmonious and bends with the needs of others, never subsuming and never overtaking. A quiet, subtle power resembling that of a butterfly, extravagant and born out of a process of transformation, of sheer will to be alive, and to be the most beautiful creature on earth.

Therein lies the power. Transformation. One cannot unearth the beauty without digging down deep to the core of your being.

Chapter 3
Unearthing

There is a beauty in digging. Digging into the earth. One never knows what it will find, what treasures lay beneath and how far one may go to find it all. This, is the mystery of unearthing, unfolding all that is within us and all that came before us, in this lifetime and in all others. The truth is, one does not actually need to start. It starts for you, digs for you, maneuvering, releasing, resting. Then the dig begins again. A new treasure, a new meaning, a new realization of what was, is or could be. There is no obvious route other than the one presented for you, each day.

The process of unearthing is not just about finding yourself or one's purpose but to see what truths lay beneath each event, each person, each happening such that your eyes may become open to the never-ending possibilities of life itself. The many meanings and beliefs that we carry, influencing every interaction and every choice. It is here, in the unearthing, that we connect with the emotion beneath the surface allowing it to be seen, felt, heard, smelt, and finally released.

On releasing, where there was trauma and pain, there is a greater understanding of why it had to stay with us until we were ready to see it. With awareness comes understanding. Of human beings, of choices, beliefs, times, and eras of society that influence what we can or cannot do and the burning desire not to choose that again. To choose differently, to be different, for the betterment of ourselves, our children, and generations beyond.

There is a story once told to me by an elderly man who was nearing retirement. He said the only way out of anything is through it, getting to the heart of what truly matters. And the most important part is to learn and grow along the way, with one heart and one mind.

This story was not about trials and tribulations. It was about *how* we undertake the work, with the awareness that we are all connected in heart and mind and what you reap you shall sow for yourself and others. There is no end to the harm that can be made to the human collective, and there is no end to the good that can be brought. It is a matter of choice. The distinction here is that intention towards the greater good of self and others is paramount. There will be hurt even where the choice is for the highest good. There is more hurt when we choose to avoid hurting others while sacrificing the highest good of self.

This cannot be mistaken for selfishness, as this is where undue harm is created out of self-righteousness and power over others. On the opposite end is selflessness, a breaking down of one's power through the belief that holding others higher is the highest good. This only serves to betray the soul by placing others in greater importance. There is no presence more important than that of your own soul, to guide you in your journey.

The continual disregard of your soul acts to fragment it, pieces breaking off, left in those spaces, places, and times of self-rejection. Over time, the remnants of your soul ache for its pieces. Searching, coping, hiding out of fear it will be further broken down. This is the dimming of the light, the light within you.

Chapter 4
The Divine Within

Within each of us there is a space of knowingness. A silence deep within us that knows the way and shows the way. In the midst of chaos and burning the midnight oil, we fail to hear this knowing, for there is chaos in our bodies generated by the will to succeed. A chaos like no other. It perpetually fuels itself until we have achieved what we desire, yet we are left unfulfilled, unsettled, wanting more. More than this, more than the other. This fuel never runs out so long as we feed it with the empty goals we strive for in current times. Making meaning for which there is none.

Would life go on if you did not achieve said goal? Of course, you would, and no one would notice. It is here that one must look at the purpose of our goals.

What do they serve?

Who do they serve?

Is it for the highest good, or for some other purpose rooted in glory, pride, shame, fear, or better yet—a self-fulfilling prophecy?

That we will be better having accomplished that goal. But will you be—truly?

Will that be what you are remembered by? Or, will it simply perpetuate a longing for more.

Would you be good enough if you had not achieved that goal? Of course you would have. We are all perfect within. We simply fail to see it and fail to hear the words that are telling us to walk slower, gentler, reminding us that there is nowhere to go but here and now.

The word peace or peaceful, can be misunderstood as meek, quiet, and lacking joy and exuberance for life. To the contrary, peace allows more of these to be present in your space. **By removing the frenetic pace by which we currently live you resonate with the higher vibrations of life that are more easily felt when your being is held in a space of calm.** Like attracts like. The well-known Law of Attraction. Being at peace does not mean resolving to a life with monks in the hillside or retreats with the yogi community. It means selecting a pace of life that is harmonious to your nature—equilibrium—or balance. Within and without.

Some may say that their nature is that of the hare rather than the turtle. But, is that truly so? Or is that a conditioning of childhood, of society, that to be sitting idle is being lazy and unproductive, and nothing good shall come from one who doesn't *do*. We have lost the art of *being*. Being with ourselves, being with others, being with nature. So much so that we consider nature retreats a form of wellness rather than embedding nature in our daily routines. From spas to yoga camps, these serve only to momentarily bring our nervous systems down a notch rather than to its base, most adaptive level. What is required of us is a slowing down on a permanent and long-term basis, allowing our inner voice and wisdom to come through.

For those unacquainted with their inner voice, or who are suspicious of and disregard what is said to be intuition, I highly recommend finding a space where you can remain in peace and undisturbed quiet for a minimum of 72 hours. This may sound ridiculous, but how many cannot bear to be with themselves for an hour much less 72?

How do you think your inner voice feels when it cannot get airtime with you because you feel others' opinions or expectations are more important than yours?

How must it feel that you have come to a place of needing others to the point you cannot bear to be with yourself?

Codependency surround us. People, places, things. **Yet the one we depend on the least is ourselves. The one we trust the least is ourselves.**

So how can we begin to trust others, to receive others when we have detached from our own inner wisdom to the point where we reject that it even exists? How do we move from codependency to interdependency—one in which our needs and desires are supported by others but are also not reliant on them? A mutual harmonious recognition that our soul's work requires first and foremost a dedication to self followed by a belief and understanding that we are better as a whole, with each soul fulfilled in the same way as our own.

There is much to learn from other beings on this planet that have for as long as they have been in existence are attuned to their surroundings, the subtle energies that make up this earthly existence. From the bears who hibernate with the season, an internal clock that keeps a watchful eye on the harvesting needs, the bounties that are needed to sustain himself through his period of rest. The period of rest is also one of regrowth, of rebirth, as the quietness settles around him. A summoning of spirits to which he rests with and a calming of the souls who will begin their journey back to earth once again. This period is pivotal in the interconnectedness of all beings. One plays a part in the other one's dance. An intricate recital of perfection as we intended right from the start.

And in the same manner in which the bear hibernates to rest with souls, as does your being require rest in order to reconnect with soul. In the spiritual sense, this is guidance we are taught to look for while in prayer, in seance, in whatever religious manner has been described is a reaching for and welcoming of your own soul, your own guidance, your own answers for which to live by.

The concept of God is across all religions in some form, yet they speak of God as someone external to you. And in this manner, it has created an expectation that someone outside of us, separate from us, holier than us will resolve our internal needs. This misconception has perpetuated the notion that our own insight has less value and that the laws or rules of religion reigns supreme. They are only as good as the gentleman who interpreted them, colored by their very own haze of conditions and beliefs.

Nowhere is there a truer representation of God's word than within you.

For within, you are God, and God is you.

Chapter 5
The Soul at Work

Seemingly random events happen when we are not paying attention. However, are they truly random? Is it random that what we think will take place will not come to be? Or, that moment we stepped onto the sidewalk and met the most important person in our life. How is it that there is no plan to the world, but it unfolds meticulously each and every day, from the sunrise to sunset, from the birth of a child with all of its bodily functions working harmoniously together, without instructions, without a person (so to speak) in the driver's seat.

We are a magnet for that which belongs to us. Our mothers and fathers chosen by us based on the soul family that we belong to, a part of our soul's journey to become all that we can be in each and every lifetime we have here on the planet. Is it miraculous that we have so many people here, never setting eyes upon millions yet the ones we do feel like home, like family, like there could be no others meant more for us than they.

These are the fabrics that make us whole, the patterns, the textures, the interweaving of lifetimes, experiences, memories upon memories that never cease to exist. This interweaving plays an important role in humanity and the evolution of us as spirit beings, for there can be no wrongdoing that cannot be made into a glorious quilt with the right intentions and the learnings from our misdeeds. It is true that karma will remain until such time that the lesson is learned, but stains fade over time, as do quilts.

The repairs that are made is what is important, the adjustments made to prevent it from recurring. **Thou shalt not fear what has been learned and forgiven, for thou shall be wiser to do no harm when the situation arises again.** There cannot be mistakes where our role as souls are to learn, for what would there be to learn if we had all the answers to begin with.

The manner in which one accepts the nature of the Universe will influence their predisposition to seemingly random events being not so random. Hear me out. How often do you learn something new and seemingly out of nowhere it is in plain sight all around you. It is not as though it did not exist previously, rather, you were just not aware of it. Awareness becomes the key. Paying attention to the patterns, the intricacies, the order amongst chaos that exists at all levels of the planet—from the mycelium in the earth to the stars and the planetary influences within and across solar systems. These are no mistakes.

The Universe seeks order and harmony across its systems, thereby aligning each to their highest potential. Why would disharmony be advantageous to the system as a whole? It would not, it would implode. And so, with each profound change that humans make to their planetary existence, a shift is required somewhere else to balance the scales. Out of sight is not out of mind. There is record of these at a minute level within the fabric that we weave. History does not repeat itself if we are careful in how we clean up the mess. To do so haphazardly will result in the same outcome.

Chapter 6
Destiny and The Destined

Perhaps where the most confusion lays is within our innermost feelings of what we are destined to be versus what we are destined for. Our destiny is our innermost value, our truest being, our nature. That, at its core, is what we are meant to be on the earthly plane. Where one *decides* to go is destined for failure unless it coincides with their internal destiny. This is not to be confused with whether what we do is good or bad; it is about our unique predisposition to carry out a certain line of work or forte of some sort that has meaning beyond the grand foreplay of life itself.

It is the essence of your core that takes you where you need to go, not the doings and accomplishments of daily life. This doingness can lead us off track if it is not in keeping with our essence of being, our truest nature. One could say that without essence one has no direction, no purpose. It is often however, a misplacement of effort and focus that carries us away from what our true purpose is. A meandering aimlessly in search of something but not seeing what is blatantly in front of us—within us—deep in our core, because we fail to hear it.

We fail to hear our own grievances, our own whispers of intention, pursuing glamour and fame instead. The ways of society rather than our own unique way. From the time we are born we are told what to be, what to do, how to behave, what is right and what is wrong. Leaving very little room for those whispers to come through. There was a time when solitude was relished but now is a sign of an introvert, the hermit, someone who doesn't belong with the rest. Different. But what is different is the access to wisdom that these individuals have.

Wherever you look there are signs, messages for you and your journey. An intricate web of goings-on that must align to get them there, but they do. There is a sophistication in the network unlike the human's straightforward thought process; there are numerous avenues for which one simple thought can make magic happen on the other side of the earth for some other being. Recognize these signs and the world is your oyster. Bringing to you every wish and every desire imaginable. As you read this book there is already the workings of your next dream—or nightmare—taking place.

The flipside of desire is fear—that which we can tolerate the least and yet we consume so much time pondering our own demise. What good would that do, to think of and plan our worst outcome, only to set in motion the steps one by one that are required for it to take place. You see, the lines of communication are so open that it would be impossible to determine if that thought was truly what you wanted because of the force and the energy behind it. You put it in motion. The notion of positive thinking is somewhat flawed, however; for it requires not only for you to think it via the mind but also to more deeply desire it, which comes from the soul. **The nature of fear can override that message of the soul if we allow it to do so. Speak only from your soul and thou shall receive.**

Be careful what you wish for when ego is in the way. There is a fine line between ego and soul when it comes to love. The bones can feel love and that is what the soul awaits. For the bones tell the story, for they are centuries old, recording history within so that your body does not forget. Where does blood come from? Your bones. Marrow. The storage-house of memories within the cellular level.

Carried through the body by blood these memories will lodge themselves until it is their time to be reviewed, reconciled, and released once and for all. The amount of memories held within our body can triple the load we must carry if we do not regularly bring to the surface these for release, or get stuck in the habit of burying new traumas and memories of this life, further compounding the burden we carry.

Receiving messages from the grid becomes challenging when the space that once existed within the crevices of our bones is no longer able to receive new messages. The bone structure is dense with memory but should be light as a feather, breathing light fragments in and out through its porous structure. The more weight that can be lifted, the greater the ability to absorb light and codes within us.

The codes are longtime known but not a well understood phenomenon due to the lengthy evolution period to achieve the insight into our own bodies, and the power they hold to heal and evolve itself. The human collective has not fully attained this ability with the exception of a certain few who were finding their way out of density and into a true light form that can no longer do harm or receive harm.

It is these beings that will transform themselves from the inside out and teach others. It is these beings that will protect you when needed, guide you, and lead you to your own transformation. There will be skeptics and critics, and those who consider themselves to be a teacher, but not all who claim to have released sufficient density to accept the challenge. To know in true form is by their language. The language of light.

Chapter 7
Demons

There is much talk about the demons inside of us but little to be said about why and how they exist. In the gothic era, demons were shown to be valuable in transmuting souls who had lost their way, forcing them to see themselves as the true light that they are by taking them to the depths of despair. In that place, they could finally see that they were just an illusion, their fears straying off course and wreaking havoc on the mind. By themselves, demons are nothing more than a fear with a face. But where demons are repeatedly fed more and more of what they thrive upon the greater and darker they become. Feasting on every part of the psyche until reaching your soul, by which point it is a mere glimmer.

At this stage, the soul has one of two options. Take an exit out of their feeble existence or remember who they truly are. It is those souls that take a chance at remembering themselves that will grow the most in their lifetime and avoid having to repeat the experience in a future life.

Demons are not harmful in and of themselves. In fact, they serve a purpose to reflect back to us parts that we must look at, what troubles us the most, and where we may find the most peace by resolving the turmoil within ourselves. To avoid our demons is like avoiding our bills. They grow, they pile, they nag and sometimes bring us to our knees.

With slow and steady attention to keep them manageable we avoid being overwhelmed and overtaken. This can be seen as the means to an end. **Pay yourself attention to what requires attention**, and it will in turn serve you well. The utmost worst you could do is wallow and have tea with them, soaking your cookies in brandy that will make them look sweeter the more you entertain them. Misery loves company. Take great care to learn from them but not let them move in.

At times the weight can be too much to bear and the soul chooses to end their journey by way of allowing such demons to consume them. This is commonly known as victimhood, whereby the physical body impersonates that this is not their choosing; but deep down they need a new start. For whatever reason that is the soul's choice. It is informed and well acquainted with the consequences of their actions. The choice is always yours even if you do not feel as though you are the one choosing. The selection of exit points has much to do with timing and the placement of possibilities within our reach. Since there are no mistakes or chances left to be taken, the only route out is through whatever means is most available to you.

For most of us a demon exists often out of sight but not out of mind. Helping someone through this dark and torturous period can seem unbearable and unattainable; however, the moment the soul remembers its light, of where it came, there is always a chance that enough strength of light can be found to burn through the dark. The demons only seek to be seen and heard, truly and deeply. Their wisdom can bring understanding to parts of us that we cannot bear to look out, shame that holds us back from our truest nature or that which we do not love ourselves. **It gnaws because it is important. So important to the health of our soul that the attention necessary is strong enough to cause harm because we no longer trust and see our own selves.**

In the end it is *us* against ourselves. No one else, but ourselves.

We are our own worst enemy.

Chapter 8
The Coming Home

To come home is a special moment. It represents a long journey from a place of warmth in the womb to the rough and dark nature of the outer world. Seemingly at odds with each other. You can't be out there and inside at the same time. Or can you?

There is a special place in between places—it represents the space of known and unknown, here and there, present and omnipresent. The space from which you have access to all but nothing at the same time. Where you once were is no longer and the future has not yet arrived. It is called the present—both the moment that is now, as well as the gift that we also define in the same term. The moment. The gift. Both are simply present. The seemingly random moments are all wrapped up in one big present—*here*.

In trying to be anywhere but here we miss the opportunity for those moments to gather momentum, to bring force behind the one thing that is all important in your soul journey—the coming home to your truest self. No more hiding, no more searching, no more weakening to the forces of the outer world. For the inner world has created its presence known across the grid and there will be no more missed opportunities, wrong choices, or wishful thinking. There will only be clarity in each and every moment that is presented to you. Divinely guided, of service to you. Everything you need shall be provided to help you along the way. No more suffering, no more drama, no more pain. You have served the earth simply by doing the work to come home to yourself. Your divine being.

Granted to you are the enormous possibilities that exist in the spiritual realm, offering you the support you need at each step of the way. **Your purpose unfolds for you when the timing is right not because there is a hold on your spirit, but because there is a need to place each part in the order in which is required.** Improper placement would be counterproductive. The timing is precise to your return to self because this is where your purpose is stored. Within your center-most core of your being. To be unlocked requires there to be enough evolution of self to recognize that which must be undertaken. The responsibility is immense, critical to the path of humanity.

You may ask where are all these people who have found their purpose and why are they not announcing it to the world? It is a deeply private matter. One of self-reflection, of pain and sorrow. And then, finally, that glimmer of hope that one is through the worst. Yet what is to come is not yet clear and to rejoice is to sound the alarm on a product not yet revealed. Pre-emptively expanding into the world will no doubt end in a premature exclusion from the world that needs it the most. The chance to embark on the divine purpose must be done with great care to avoid sacrificing the very vessel in which it resides and travels through.

To be divinely guided means there is trust in something grander, trust that you are fully and without doubt carried through each and every part of your life for the single purpose to find love.

This is no ordinary love.

The divine love is one of reverence, of depth, of soul-shattering quality that exudes a warmth and care for some other as equal to their own. Their regard for this love is primacy, its sole purpose to balance the scales of feminine and masculine, to correct the harms done by prior unsuccessful love matches, and return the soul fragments back to the soul. The recognition of souls is seemingly benign until the song which has intertwined the two for centuries upon centuries ignites the soul space. This song of the heart echoes and resounds a frequency only heard by these souls. Breaking through the very matrix that has kept them apart, restoring synchrony to their souls.

The feeling of reuniting may be one of pureness. Of knowing without knowledge. Of familiarity without having the foundation of which to frame in. Of seeing, deeply within their innermost feelings without a word being shared. The sensory overload that may arise is caused by the flood of energy across realms, dimensions, lives, and times for which you have existed. A shattering of boundaries between space and time. There is no such thing in the lives of these souls upon reuniting. There is only one place where they exist. Within.

To arrive at this place jointly is essential to the soul's future work together in support of their own life purpose and that of each other. Their combined mission. Combined mission has the greatest potential to revive the lost harmony across souls. The level of power generated through union has the ability to replenish, restore, and reignite souls depleted by the current state of the world and manners in which we live. The restoration will accelerate growth at a time that is paramount for karma to be resolved in the collective. For balancing the scales in the collective masculine and feminine energy for the purpose of renewing trust, hope, and love. Within and without.

Make no mistake. When you find the love of your life, you shall know, you shall see, you shall hear across time and space. You shall not be without because they are within forever more. Amen.

Chapter 9
The Golden Hour

Time has meaning, time has essence. There are moments in time that cannot be undone. This is the power we have over each moment, second, minute that rests within the palms of our hands. Unseen, precious, precarious, all-encompassing. These are the days of our lives all folded into one precious atom resting within our souls. There is no time they say; but, time will run out if you allow it to. Eternity is for souls, but for the being that reads this, time must take on a new meaning from before.

The concept of time historically allowed peasants to be monitored for their productivity, captive from the freedom of their once non-existent fairytale dream, they say. Horticulture depends on time—the hours of sunlight offered to a seedling is what creates its abundance.

But what if time had new meaning in the existential question of what is the purpose in life?

What if time is merely an opportunity to gauge our rest-to-work ratio that can give us our likelihood of succeeding at evolution, not based on what we produce, but on the hours of rest, thus allowing creation to form. Without rest, productivity takes more effort, more energy, and therefore less effect overall.

The rest-to-work ratio was once admired by kingdoms who lavished in their abundant fields, fragrant flowers and plethora of dancing in the moonlight. This energy of life—joie de vivre—instilled greater joy in the art of doing, making the basic harvest or fix an enjoyable one. Those were the days of reaping what you sow and reaping some more. High quality garments were a sign of prosperity for both owners and workers alike, never seeking to see those less than or above status at a par level higher.

Higher integrity of our relationship with things and people allows for a respectful exchange, having enough, but no more than one needs. This is balance in goods. In equal form is a balance in fair wage, honor within the workforce, and pride amongst society for that which is earned and paid. Pride of ownership, of skill, and place in society all serve to uphold a non-class system that recognizes the rights and responsibilities of all members of society. Beholden are we to find those arts and systems once again.

Why, one would ask, is this key to one's journey to love? What have we to garner from the same story as it applies to love? That there can be no power imbalance if there is to be a reciprocal exchange of energy within oneself and with a soul partner. Each soul must respect the value the other brings and return to it a mutual offer of energy in the form of love, kindness, respect, support for one's personal journey, and partake in the mission of the joint souls. There is no greater mission of two souls than this. **Where one can find balance within themselves, they have greater potential**

within the joint mission to honor and respect the needs of balance in the other.

In the offer of balance to relationship, there is a trust that can be formed, allowing space for creating, co-creating, exemplifying love bonds that cross centuries. And the making of these bonds is true alchemizing of wounds and traumas within the grid of the soul family and across families. The souls of such bonds are irrevocably tied to one another for their mission is to maintain this balance and trust within the system in order for alchemical processes to take place. Their separation can create great harm to the female soul who seeks to be grounded in the strength and power of the male for her purpose to unfold successfully and without undue delays. There must be reciprocity for this to occur.

Vibrant partnerships occur when there is a willingness to step equal distance into the trenches and darkness, to amend the wrongdoings of past karma that continues to affect both souls, to reform those soul bonds through intentional and thoughtful actions that will reaffirm their commitment to the whole. With no awareness of the value these have, the journey will struggle until each soul has learned these values towards themselves and towards each other.

Chapter 10
The Cauldron

It was once said that where there is animal bones there is great strength to beholden from the waters that boil it broken. From here the story tells of the nourishment in the centermost core, the marrow, where all life's records are kept. Cellular memory.

In the blood cells, the mitochondria perform an important role in keeping the cellular memory intact. The cells travel through the body, depositing fragments into the muscles and fascia to be released overtime. There is exponential fragments carried in certain blood-rich organs such as the heart and liver, where mitochondria naturally perform their development and evolution through the body. From home to waste. These are the central places in which we carry the hardest of memories, those related to love and fear. It is no wonder the pain these organs endure through lifetimes of heartbreak and negative karma, reaping their effects through jealousy, loss, anger and rage.

It is here, in these organs, that life begins as a growing fetus, the beginnings of its own life support system already mired by the generational trauma from past lives, ancestral bloodlines and the experiences of the mother who holds so precariously this *blob* of cells destined for greatness. If only it had a chance to heal before another life ensues.

The quest for healing is not new. The Romans invented spa baths for such purpose, incentivized by the impressive columns and sculptures that evoke strength and angelic guidance along one's journey to heal. The process was flawed however, in the fact that the individual must partake in the witnessing of the wound. Romans were far too stoic.

The Egyptians created temples of love to surround themselves in God's light while releasing demons through various forms of tinctures and womb-cleansing performed by medicine women of the time. These women were known for their healing attributes—a warming of the hands when touched, glazed-over eyes as they harnessed spirits, and a gothic look to ward off the demons. Countless records depict these skills, yet the rulers of the day denounced that they exist.

From medieval times there are witches and warlocks with special seances to rid the body of evil pasts and the tendencies to 'wipe' the body clean while doing so. This is thought to be a force that detaches from the soul-spirit in the process.

Western knowledge has failed to recall these important wisdom-keepers, like yourself, for the prime reason in that it fails to acknowledge the existence of soul-spirit. These are used interchangeably at this point because spirit has at least become to have place within the psycho-social constructs of religion and spiritually-based practices such as yoga, qigong, tai chi and Hindu bhakti.

These practices are rooted in one's spirit, life force, or prana, which have similar meaning to spirit–breath, respire–*spiritus* in Latin. These foundations of the movement of and nurturance of the body with an unseen presence continues to befuddle western science. The concept of a soul even more so.

To tell one's soul exists requires only the presence, calmness, and a willingness to look inside. Failing to have all three will not create the container for soul to speak. Where one feels their life force dimming is also a sign that the container is broken. The vessel or container of one's body hosts the space of life within the lower third of the body–the place of the womb of creation, the stomach and spleen reforming energy from food, and the intestines which digest and expel unused or unwanted energy. These systems must function efficiently for the qi to not stagnate and prevent a build-up of external harmful energy. In perfect function, this cauldron of organs sustains life force and gives energy to other vital organs. Without this life force is a draining of the entire system as a whole.

If we look at the stressors of modern-day life, there is extensive knowledge of the detrimental impacts, yet we fail to act on them for the betterment of ourselves and our society. The lives lost through obesity and diabetes alone are staggering. The depressive states caused by allergens, toxins–both inadvertent and intentional–act to disrupt the body's natural functions. Where one part of the car is misfiring, so shall the car fail to run properly. Longstanding issues such as fibromyalgia are rooted in a dysfunction of the metabolic system thus causing widespread ailments that are difficult to draw conclusive evidence for a particular cause.

We draw our attention back to the bones, the calcium-rich broth that re-establishes the metabolic system and the endocrine system from the ferric-rich collagen. From here we have a chance of rebalancing the digestion and thyroid system. Glands that previously stopped functioning due to excess hormones can now restart.

This, is the meticulous construct we call the human body but fail to respect the artform that it is. Precious, fragile yet resilient, functioning in perfect harmony. If only we would allow it so.

Chapter 11
The Heart of it All

Alone in the world we feel but the heart knows beyond limits of our own body and that which we place upon it. The heart feels, provides, feels, provides. That is its only job. To sense the needs of the mind and the vascular system in order to respond to the stressors that we must endure on this earthly planet. There is no discourse however. It simply is. The discourse results in our mind in how it portrays events to be.

From the moment of birth, the heart knows beyond a shadow of a doubt that it is loved beyond measure. That the mother's force has greatly brought it into its being and forever more is connected by way of heart resonance, the truest of love at the heart of mother and child. The art of heart resonance continues to develop with each and every being in which the child encounters, either on a soul level or a physical level.

There is the recognition at a soul level within the heart when one remembers a part of its former lives, a spark ignites within it, setting off chemical reactions to warm, center, and hone that feeling so as to not lose it through its life on earth. The chemical reactions at the neuron level assure the memory, the scar within the tissue, is forever embedded in the body. There are lifetimes of scars that are remembered during the course of your life that serve to refocus you at times most needed. To keep you on course of your truest path.

At the child stage these are easiest to endure because the child mind is so easily adaptable and responsive to its inner guidance or intuition. As time moves on, this inner guidance is meant to be cultivated for the pursuit of greatness and wholeness, and responsive to the evolutionary needs of human beings. **There is not one piece of guidance that is wrong, for the Universe shows exactly what is out of alignment and what must be corrected to bring us back on course.** Like an intricate map that all directions and paths lead us home, the heart functions as this map, solely for the purpose of our greatness, our grace, our fullest, calmest, most elaborate coming into being and presence of soul.

There must be space made for that connection to heart be made strong and unwavering in the midst of chaos. There must be a presence to heart and that which it is responding to, the stimuli, and what it means for you as a person living a physical life. The heart will respond favorably to options most suited to its happiness and growth, neutral where it either delays or impedes growth, and, unequivocally sore when the actions will cause great pain and harm to the being in some way, form, the timing of which is indicated by the strength of the sore.

Pain of the heart should never be ignored. This is a sign of impending heartache and misery for which can and will occur if corrections are not made. The heart leads in these circumstances to set off an internal movement of malaise through the body to 'make' it stop, slow down, and pause for the resonance and the connection to take place within you. There is nothing like an illness to reset your thinking and meaning for life. This is the hearts doing, the hearts way of reminding you that you are great and that great things will come if you allow it to lead the way.

Pulses of the heart will weaken when it sees danger, a withdrawing of life force to protect it from that which is not of its highest potential. This is different than the fear–fight or flight–mode in which the heart races to gain momentum to its reaction. The withdrawal of heart force is in response to a negative or less than ideal option to pursue. For the being to continue along this path will require considerable expenditure of energy to keep going. It is not backed by the love-induced heart energy that is built when thriving and supporting the true path.

In contrast, the thriving heart is one of life, of excitement, of a heart filled with warmth and joy that it overflows the pores of the body. This is the typical light of love which can be felt and seen when two people in love are free to allow their heart to speak, unfiltered, freely flowing in both directions. This is what the heart pursues and requires to maintain harmony in the body and soul for the purpose of its path. The deviation from path will lead one down a heartless road to non-existence in the eyes of the soul.

To exist is to be in love, and to love is to be following the eyes and mind of the soul. There cannot be love where the path is not freely on its journey. Fraught are those who deny themselves of this existence, where heart is not only the source but refinement of love, the guiding star, the true north of one's journey. Blinded by the external promises of shimmering solutions to our internal dilemmas when all we have to do is look inside, feel inside, and respond to the messages and direction that are, and have always been, available to us.

There can be no wrong way when our hearts lead the way.

Chapter 12
The View of the External World

How we view ourselves in relation to the external world has a profound effect on where we shall find ourselves in each moment. If we are not cognizant of our place in the world and our true potential to do and be great, we will continue to limit ourselves and take a small seat within the sphere of influence in our life and that of others. Where there is willingness to step into the shoes of our power, there is a channel of power and supply that is readily accessible to the fulfillment of the path. There is no need to effort, to work, when the work is being done through pure potential and commitment to the internal journey of the soul.

There is no greater source of energy than from the divine power of Source energy, the powerhouse of our beingness. Simply put, **the Source is your power to fulfill your destiny and can only be accessed when you have realized your place in the world and the purpose you serve for all of humanity**. For these people, power and energy are limitless, the tools and means to accomplish its work are provided by the Universe and all other beings who have attained this realization. This is self-actualization, the place in which we create our destiny from a place of knowing, of trusting, of faith, of harmony with oneself and within the whole of humanity. This is what the soul seeks, longs for. The truest path.

Imagine if all souls were on their path to self-actualization? Where would greed, wars come from if there were no energetic powers to feed those ways of being. There would be only love, for self and others. A harmonious existence amongst soul families, recognizing the needs of our brothers and sisters to enable their greatest potential. Resolving disputes harmoniously because the heart knows and is trusted to its fullest extent. There is a space within this structure that allows for self while supporting others and honoring of one's own purpose, while convening as a whole and recognizing where there is self-actualization or greed at play. When one serves the whole through self-actualization, there can be no greed because the benefit is not for self, it is for all of humanity.

It is when ego gets in the way, beliefs and self-made agreements that fulfills their own prophecy of being selfless while serving no purpose for others, or serving a harm to others. Selfless qualities are done for the purpose of "appearance" of outward value, how one looks in the face of others, how one will be regarded if actions A or B are taken. Not of regard for the soul and its purpose. For the soul has no other purpose but to serve humanity. And that is the greatest gift we can give to serve our soul first and foremost, such that it can provide for humanity in all its forms. Mental, spiritual, emotional, and physical.

These forms have evolved based on our own human constructs but ultimately reflect the body's capacity to feel, see, and understand its multisensory and multidimensional experiences and to reinvest these experiences into the needs of humanity. The needs of humanity is fraught with opinions rather than a baseline fundamental expression of our true capacities to live and breathe in a manner that is self-supporting and free of harm to others. **This notion that our evolution requires us to consume or overtake another species, to be the almighty, the power versus subservient, is not founded in love and harmony.**

Harmony exists when we each are offered the opportunity to live our purpose until our purpose is fulfilled. And then our soul chooses a new adventure. When we are not offered the opportunity to fulfill this purpose at the explicit notion that another being is granted greater authority over us is not a notion built from love and honor of each soul. It is built upon a history of power and greed, of the masculine era. One that has even consumed the power of the feminine to the extent that the feminine power has no room to balance, to rest in her beauty, submissive to the hunger for achievement of society rather than a fulfillment of soul and heart.

A failure to support the needs of the collective feminine has only one road to travel–to more greed, power, war, and heartache. At the center of this heartache will be the root of all illness, death, and disease. A relentlessness preoccupation with fixing "it" rather than fixing ourselves and our role within the whole. A belief that we can manage our way through diseases of the heart will only continue the ache that leads us there.

The solution?

Heart-centered therapies that enable the return back to self, back to soul. A remembrance of why we are here, why we exist, how we are to be on our path, our place as a soul within the whole.

Chapter 13
Access to Wisdom

There is a truth which lies beneath all actions and inaction. A truth which cannot be hidden, ought not to be hidden, and will make itself known to those who must see it. Where there are secrets there is a hidden need to be seen, to be truly honored as a being, a soul, that has purpose and a greater meaning within the world.

To remain hidden is to be silenced, to be restrained from greatness, withheld from gracing your light upon those who need it the most. This, leading to despair amongst those that need your gifts to realize their own. There is no purpose to hiding that which can be of benefit to the world.

Our need to remain hidden is fear-based. A fear of our true potential and where it may take us. Fear of the unknown, unseen, unheard. Our childhood has fostered this, a reluctance to step into the circle, of being at the center for all to see.

What this generates is a fear of expectation, a failure if one does not succeed. Of the mind, this fear can impede even the strongest of souls from beginning their purpose. Conditioned to be minimal, or adequate, or just enough to be accepted within the group of the majority.

What we never seem to realize soon enough is that the majority are downplaying their greatness; therefore, we as a collective are not living or seeing the truth of our nature. The collective is reticent to acknowledge their abilities and strengths bestowed upon them to the point we live meaningless lives.

Work, eat, sleep. Work, eat, sleep. Work, eat, sleep.

Let that sink in. How much excitement can your soul gain from this existence? None. Lackluster, life-suppressing. All in the auspices of societal expectations of place in class, dogma, and the wrongful deeds of our ancestors.

It is now time for these secrets to be seen, to be heard. For truths to awaken our level of existence, our shadows, demons, and history that continues to repeat itself. **Our rightful places as souls is not to remain hidden, for our existence as humanity depends upon it. It depends upon our willingness to see and accept the truth and to take actions towards self-realization and our highest purpose.**

These are the only actions to be taken. They are simple but feared by many.

Chapter 14
Understanding the Truth

Truth [what is true] represents the sum of all possibilities. It is not a matter of perception or opinion. It is. The possibilities are endless, but they all amount to the same thing at the final point of all beingness–an expression of yourself that wishes to be realized amongst the vastness of the Universe. The expression that will resonate across the grid for benefit of all beings, without doubt or detrimental harm, it will occur. Mark my words. The truth is what we are seeking, amongst each other and ultimately for ourselves. A state of being in accord with our potential, our purpose, our knowingness.

Failure to see the truth is what creates unrest amongst ourselves and each other. Take the discord amongst wars, a classic display of preventing the truth from being told, for doing so would give the other side advantage, a view into the vulnerable side of the fleet, a crack in which the authority one has upon the other can break down the guard and permit intrusion by outside forces.

This is the same fear that evades us now. The fear of intrusion into our most sensitive parts, our shadows, our gifts, our habits, and preferences, all of which can and has been used against us. The wall that we place around these not only creates division but a protection around that which gives us strength, resilience, ultimate power over our own destiny. When we choose how these are used and with whom, we create a system of better and best, access/denial, have/have not. This perpetuates more of the same rationing of our ability to trust in others. The more we protect the less we trust.

The more we have to offer, the more generous the offering in return. **The more adept we are at trusting life's processes, like the rising of the sun and setting of the moon, will we be able to trust the truest nature of each other.** The truth is that we all have generous gifts to give, that we are kind and gentle in the heart, and what matters is that we have allowed this to show. By protecting that which is our most valuable asset we fail to thrive.

Protection is a word that harbors great meaning to the soul. It instills fear, the fight and flight mechanism. And so it goes into hiding. Resurrecting the soul from continuous need of protection is futile, for it will not emerge until the guards are fully dropped, hands held open to the world for every beautiful and deserving moment that comes our way. In this light, there is no need for protection. Only for discernment in how we respond to the moment, how we learn from it, and to whom we owe the blessings of our soul.

For there are more precious moments than one could conjure up, yet we focus primarily on those that may cause harm, whether they are bound to occur or not. Existence is futile if all we see is the negative associations of that which surrounds us. Like attracts like. And so, the circle of life continues until we break out of our morbid view of the world and the circumstances that we find ourselves.

Holding at the center of our being is the chakra *ananda*, the powerhouse of our being, our will, our ability to express who we are and why we are here[1]. This center point is foundational to who we are and our will to take steps towards our soul's mission. An unchecked power center, one will remain confused, a state of non-knowing, unsure, aimless and without direction, for they seek guarantees of their safety and happiness when there is none. Until we find our soul that is.

When we re-establish the connection with our soul is when we have assurances that only we can see and know. These assurances is what propels us to do and try more, to trust, to worry less, and aim high.

No more waiting and wondering. There is a sureness, a contemplated awareness, that all will be well.

---

1. It is important to note that the chakras as humans have defined them are equating them only as energies rather than their innate expression of being. Innate expression is not an energy, it is a modus operandi, a state, of pure harmony within, expressed as divine will and grace, of seeking our truest nature of being.

Chapter 15
Becoming

Becoming acquainted with yourself again takes time, to nourish, to nurture those parts of the soul that have been pre-emptively hidden. To hide is to be ignored, to be abandoned and abolished to abysmal conditions. A lack of self-worth will further deteriorate the soul's ability to recover and resume its functions towards harmony and wholeness. The heart-centered approach to living will reignite the spirit and allow the soul space to come forward on its renewed path and soul journey. The faded spirit takes patience and time.

Uplifting breathwork and yoga will help ignite the fire, as does joyful living with space to simply be at one with the body again, and heal those parts that have been abandoned. **To be, fully and completely, with no demands, no distractions and no recurring pain is of utmost importance in this time.** The pain caused from separation of the soul and body can be harsh, deep, and plentiful as it marks each of the layers within the central energies. Each layer requires healing in order to rebuild strength and resiliency. Incomplete healing will only serve to stifle growth and resurrection of the divine powers within.

Ensuring the soul has access to its guides and angels on a regular basis brings about an enormous potential for energy to rebuild in the body system, creating a safe space for evolution, and returning back to oneness. Harm can occur when the soul is fragile from continuous reminders of historical pain.

Withdrawing from daily activities may serve the need to retract and regenerate, integration, and alleviating what no longer serves the highest needs of the soul. Resuming these activities when guided and appropriate will assist to maintain a level of safety and compassion for the growing soul that marks its growth through shedding and releasing external layers of energy. This can be quite painful as the detaching process occurs roughly every six to 12 hours for a duration of 10 days. Laying on a comfortable platform or bed for these periods can speed up the process whilst the body is still. Consuming pure foods in bright colours will move the energy beyond the physical realm, dense to light, and further supported by digestion processes. Warming foods and elixirs stimulate digestion, as does heating the body, releasing these layers through the pores of the skin. Do not conduct heavy tasks or activities. All energy must be focused on this shedding period.

Chapter 16
A Shoulder to Cry On

Millions of years have passed and yet the result of separating from Source will continue to affect the physical body and spirit if it is not truly healed. Where one cell is healed this releases the burden and weight on others that must carry this. As we heal, one by one, the lighter the load becomes. Allowing more and more light to shine through the physical body as once existed. There is no such thing as weightless, but lighter is what we must strive for.

Bearing the history that we have placed upon us serves no purpose. It must be released from the dwelling that continues. The inability to lift ourselves from the misery of prior actions. Consciously this can take place while not redeeming those who have harmed. Rather, this makes space for a new way, new thought, more kindness. This is the way forward.

In amongst the trees, you shall find bright green growth taking place amongst the dying vegetation that has lived. From this, mycelium take the best that it has to offer and feeds its surroundings. It does not dwell on its passing—it brings strength to the new potential that exists in that moment. And in that moment, every moment, there is a point at which we choose either to take what has happened and grow from it, benefiting that which exists around us and through the whole Universe.

This network that mycelium creates is connected across vast distances. It knows the reach of its powers, and this is what drives its being. It is because it serves the whole. This is how we can see ourselves, not living for our own selfish needs and desires but having an impact on each and every living, and so-called non-living thing in this world. We touch upon it in the non-physical, in the energy that we present to the world each and every moment.

There is a quality to our being that can either help or hinder our own growth and that of others. This does not mean positivity. It means a concrete presence within ourselves and our environment that will connect across worlds and through our energetic makeup, support each other's existence. There can be no us if there is not you and me and the beings around us playing their own important role. It is within each of us to recognize this central purpose and act accordingly.

Our intentions play a big part in the success of our beingness. We can either harness the wind because it suits our own need or we can do so because we all need it. One will have greater impact on the other, subsuming the needs of one when the whole is the intention. There can be no positive outcome when the individual is the only to gain. However, this does not equate to selflessness or martyrdom where there is a complete loss of self when giving to others. For they are still being done for the purpose of self under the guise of others.

True intention of the whole recognizes that one individual's strength offers great support to the whole and by being whole and resilient as a single being is not the purpose. Self before others comes from the place of acknowledging that we cannot give from an empty cup. It is not rooted in gain for individual power or pleasure. When selfishness is at play there is a desire to be better than others, have more than others. Imbalance in power and growth for individual purpose is at play. This is ego, striving for place and power in the structure of society. Gain is for the person not the people. Individual strength must be built for resiliency of the whole, not to be of power for oneself.

Lamenting over what could be or the wrongdoings of our ancestors takes the power we have as a whole and makes it stagnant—within that place and time—not allowing for us to move past history. **The past is to be learned from not to stay in.** There is opportunity everywhere to move beyond the past if we can get out of our heads and move into our soul. The soul's nature is of growth, learning from the past, and finding a way forward. This can only be done if we know of our soul's existence and its truest nature. That of kindness, love, and prosperity as a human collective.

There once was a tale of a being that would resist help from others. He truly saw within himself that if he could break down his internal walls that he would have everything he ever needed to support his existence. He built his livelihood on internal self-reflection and learning from his own barriers that he never once required a hand-out from others. He brought to himself a place of being that understood that all would come before him when he shed the past within him. There would be room to breathe, to accept, to nourish his own soul, and the souls of others. This could not take place before he let go of anything and everything that he believed would protect him externally. Not food, not water or home, or structures or things. They were of no use if he could not rest in his own body knowing that it had everything it needed to provide sustenance and prosperity.

This, is the power of beingness that cannot be replaced by the material world. **There can be no prosperity if we cannot already see that which we are made of. There cannot be peace if we have no peace inside.** *There cannot be a higher power if we cannot see the power of our soul.*

Now, what does this all mean in terms of our soul's journey to love? Once we see the power of our soul, a whole new world opens around us. The wisdom that is accessible, the insight, the sights and sounds beyond the sensory mind. The resonance that resides within us all and how it guides us to where we need to go. Each step of the way. There is no truer expression than when we speak from our soul, when we walk with the power of our soul behind us, walking ever so closely to guide and pursue our highest potential. When we let this in we "see" that which we could not previously, the opportunities that lay before us with more clarity and visibility that there is no question in what we must do. We simply do, because we know, beyond a shadow of a doubt.

Doubt is a form of negativity that pervades our being. Bringing to question that which we know to be true, but preventing our actions. There lays behind this a deep-rooted fear of trusting our intuition, our inner voice, which is essentially our soul speaking to us. Fear of being wrong, of basing our actions on the unseen, is considered to be weak, uninformed, and irresponsible.

It is these factors that society has built that are holding us back from listening to our soul's call. Harboring more and more disdain amongst each other because this is our doing *to* each other. We cannot seem to drop the ego enough to let it break through. Allowing the remembering to take place is a threat to our current life as we know it.

Chapter 17
The Call

How long can you resist the call of the soul?

The relentless longing, expectations of the material world that never materialize, always leaving something more to be desired. That call has always been there, beckoning, blissfully waking you up each day trying to get your attention. But inevitably we fall into pattern, into routine. Creating an endless loop. Over and over again. The same dimension, the same quality. Never striving to think beyond that which is in front of us. This is not living in the moment. This is stagnancy.

Where heart meets soul is where life begins to unfold as a flower gently releasing one petal at a time. It is an unfolding of the greatest powers within you, a building of a garden that blooms because of the witnessing of something grander. A garden that beautifies the space in which we live and breathe, a space that transforms us as we transform within. Bathing us in the beauty of our own work, our own making. Brilliantly allowing the earth to support us in every step along the way. The earth that provides for us will watch us unfold in the same way that its own beauty does. *We are one of them.* One of the beautiful traits of the earth that we often do not see in and of ourselves.

There is a time when we confront ourselves, ask the tough questions. Is this it? Is there not more to this life?

There is, we just have not been listening to the deepest part of us that already knows all of these answers. Open the door. It is waiting for you. It has been waiting all along.

The answers lay deep within you. Can you muster up the strength to go there? Put all the shame and judgments aside, look them straight in the eye and acknowledge their presence but let them know that you are not them. They are not you. They are a figment of your imagination that you have created out of fear of the unknown, fear of the misplaced intentions, the harm you may have caused.

The need we have for belonging amongst others has superseded the belonging within ourselves. The importance we place on the thoughts of other people whom we do not even know. People who judge us but care less of our happiness, paramount is the happiness of their own.

Why so much power to these individuals?

How can they serve us when their intentions are not directed at us?

These are the questions that will lead us to our own knowing, our own fulfillment. This does not mean abandoning those who provide us social stimulation. It is about a rebalancing of power that they hold over us. A recognition that we each unto ourselves have a responsibility to ourselves first so that we may be of service to others. Once we have become all that we can be for ourselves is when we can lift those up around us.

Heaven belongs to all of us. The notion that some will go to hell is a falsity, a myth, developed to instill fear for the purpose of maintaining power and order over society. The church-run state can only do harm, for it is instilling beliefs that supersede our own authority, sovereignty, and individual rights of our beingness. It predisposes one to marginalization for not keeping with the established standards and relegating those who do not comply to a lesser class. Submissive and powerless we become over our own affairs, choices that are dictated by others whose beliefs are believed to be almighty.

God is not almighty. He (or she) recognizes individual strength is equal across humans, the resources for which are used may be different, but in our hearts, we are the same. Tailoring our destiny to meet a certain need, no less or more important than another. If we can see this equality across all individuals and that religion is a source of discord within and across religions, we can begin to understand the division we have created within ourselves as people.

When this awareness grabs a hold of the heart, it cannot undo what it now knows. From this place change can occur. Change can ripple from one mind to another and from one heart to another. There can be no love between ourselves if we do not see the power differences we have built within our structures. The structures will eventually fold when there is insufficient power to hold them up. This is the goal.

Now, where to begin. **Within the heart, centered over our trueness, we can speak truthfully without exception.** There will be times and places where speaking the truth may seem awkward or inappropriate, but these are the more important moments. When shifts in thought are greatest. When questions bring curiosity, thought provoking and meaningful conversations about truth, as we see it. Finding the truth is one step in the game; bringing it to others and showing the way must follow in order for change to occur. These steps will play a foundational role for those who have seen truth, stepping out of norms and comforts. It will not be easy but it can be done with willingness and connection to Source at all times and places.

Take time each day to intentionally identify a place in which change in belief needs to occur. Bring light to this intention and hold it throughout the day. No effort is needed, simply walk with it and the place will find you. Enabling your being to hold such immense power to transform can ultimately change the world if each one of us does so; over time the power will transform thought, one by one. Realizations without having direct experience, only the vibration surrounding them that will transform their state of being.

Care is needed when using this power to avoid creating new systems of hierarchy and power. Highest good must always be sought with the intention. Power must never be used for ill, harm, or direct benefit to self.

The changes from heart-inspired will can inevitably change the world around self. An inordinate amount of abundance is brought to those who transform self and the world.

There is nothing to do.

Chapter 18
The Day to Day

Day to day, we can become more present with ourselves, our soul, on a deeper level by activating our kundalini powers. There is much to be said about the awakening process and the ups and downs it creates. But there is a purpose to this and a higher power that resides within us that can serve our highest needs. And when we can harness that energy our life force becomes insurmountable. Nothing can get in its way.

The kundalini energy becomes the process of tapping into what is otherwise left silent. How it is harnessed is key to avoid symptoms of dysfunction within the body. Too much can throw one off balance, too little does not bring the body to the necessary point of brightness to activate all energy centers at the same time.

Step one is to bring the body and mind to complete stillness and non-thought. Meditation practice is important to gain this step easily. Once the mind is at ease and the body functions resting, imagine a cord connecting you to the earth's core. This centers and keeps you grounded to the physical plane while accessing the heavens. To do the process without effective grounding will result in the crown chakra opening too wide and becoming lost in the cosmos.

Step two is to bring earth force into the root chakra and the samsidara chakra which is embedded within the root chakra. This is not well known as most yogis will only connect to the larger foundational chakra. This smaller chakra creates pressure across the pelvic region that signals to the serpent an impending release, preparing it so to speak. The pressure builds its way up the main channel across the remaining chakras, opening, and signaling. Once the crown has been reached with this signal, grasp the skies with your minds eye, while remaining connected with earth. This balance and opening makes it possible for the serpent to rise with ease.

Step three, with the upper and lower chakras connected and spinning, envision a powerful light at the base of the spine where it meets the coccygeal region. Use white light to stimulate the region. As you do this, it creates a safe opening for the serpent to rise. It may be slow or quick to rise, it does not matter. The key to performing this sequence is safety and presence, or it will not rise. As the circuit begins to proceed up the spine it will correct any misalignments, unblock sections of the body that are stagnant, and release their true power and connect to Source energy. There may be feelings of bliss as this happens, an opening to heavens, or release of energy through the crown showering your body with golden fragments, elevating your body out of a slumber. The mind's eye may see visions of what is being released. This is not to be suppressed, but rather observed in order to complete the healing process of the events. There may also be sensations or a "lifting" of the body off the surface which it sits. This elevation is a sign of a true connection to Source as it strives to be in balance or centered between the heavens and earth planes, equally receiving from both. This is why it is essential to be corded to earth to avoid an out-of-body experience instead of the serpent rising.

Handle this process with care. The body can only receive so much light during the early parts of awakening and can dramatically affect mental health if done too quickly. Aim for once per month, then progress to once per week, maximum. The periods between are necessary for integration of light energy and codes or keys that are meant for you to receive throughout your life. The space allows for full release of traumas and a regaining of mental and physical clarity. It will become evident when the next connection is appropriate when there is a marked peace within the body.

Strive to nurture the soul and physical body during this process, eliminating all toxins and reducing environments. Help the process through regular rest and relaxation techniques, bright foods and beverages, subtle acupressure on the forehead, and resist the urge to process too deeply.

All that needs to rise and release will rise. Temptations linked to those events will surface. Do not engage them, for they will take root in new parts of the body and continue the cycle which is trying to be broken. Observe, breathe, release. Until it no longer is visible within your mind or body. Try to remain calm and centered as this occurs—this creates safety in the nervous system and an allowance for the fight or flight system to be usurped.

When the nervous system has been on overdrive for generations, a new process needs to be established that recognizes the sensitivity of the body to its surroundings and it's knowing deeply rooted in the soul. This knowing is what will allow a confident and appropriate response to future events. The resetting of this process is the goal.

Chapter 19
Telling the Soul's Work

There can be no mistake when the soul speaks to us. Its trueness cannot be doubted, its message coming from the core of who we are, bringing voice to the deepest needs and desires of who we are and the most quintessential parts of us that we often overlook or mistaken as lofty or unattainable. **This is a mistake, to grant authority to a society that seeks to be modest and normal over our capacity to be exceptional.**

It is attainable, it is lofty based on where we must go to reach our highest potential. It is at this lofty place where we can see the meaning of it all, the possibilities of it all. There is no sense in mediocre if our best work is done without effort in a place where self-realization is supported, nurtured, and fostered.

When we take a step back and look at progress as humanity, the big jumps in evolution are when we dared to be great. Dared to go to the moon, the depths of the sea, built coliseums by hand. Because we knew we could, and we tried. It is not without effort, but effort is relative when you have mastered the art of light. With light, there is a weightless aspect of all matter that is harnessed, that shapes us as beings and other objects.

Carrying the weight of our past in all things human and object serves no purpose than to slow us down, strain more, lift more, and extends the period we remain in the density. All of us sacrifice when we are not able to let go of that which weighs us down. From ancient ruins, wars and power strife, each embeds heaviness to our present time.

That which is light is free. It is able to move without friction across planes and dimensions; time travel becomes effortless. There is no place that you cannot go within the sphere. Chances are the blissful states of happiness have allowed you to exit and return without you even knowing. This is light, this is living in a Universe that wants you to achieve and experience all that is possible from the comforts of where you are *now*. Not in 10 years time. In *this* moment. Every moment for eternity.

Every time you experience you build another lens for which to step forward upon, a new way of seeing and thinking. These lenses obtained during travel out of your physical body are preparing you for future actions and purpose, building the skills for you to effortlessly bring that future into the now. This is multidimensional living. No effort, no harm, because all the things are brought to you as you need it.

There is nothing to do except be present and ready to accept that which is brought for you in each moment. You will know what to do when it arrives. There will be no question. **There will only be a knowing that you cannot refuse or doubt. It will eat at your core if you do not proceed and will propel you for miles when you do take that first step.**

The first step is all that you need to take.

Chapter 20
The Light in Your Heart

S hine the light into your heart and watch it grow. Watch it expand beyond your self, your space, your home, and into those around you. This expansion is called resonance, the magnetic force behind yourself, your heart, your very existence.

There is a field around you that emits exceptionally high frequencies when you expand and live in your heart center. The heart-centered concept was developed from the belief that love can heal all, love can bring us together. It is much more than that. It is an epic field of glory that is emitted when one is centered in their emotions and beingness that is unshakable and reaches the depths of one's existence, to the point it touches others beyond their imagination.

Red, rich red, is surrounded by those that embody the heart as its foundation of being. When we reside in a space of love wholly, the heart becomes a magnet to all that is wholesome and free. It is a sense of freedom yet connectedness to that which it holds most dear. The foundation within self and others is the recognition that one is not the whole and only a piece of it, yet is whole unto themselves at the same time. There is a bridge between worlds, a truth that cannot be broken amongst those who see and hold true to themselves in what and who they are.

There is a knowing, a being. **There is nothing to do.** But wait. Wait for that which is meant to be, already in existence within the Universe and destined to be present. The time in which it unfolds is a mystery but is a binding piece of reality that cannot be undone. For it is a miracle when they see the whole and a miracle when existence on earth becomes a dance in the heavens of possibilities and realities that merge upon us.

Time is an illusion, a construct for which the non-linear cannot fathom. A mind-bending surge of creation unfolds when one lets go of time fully and completely. There is no constraints, no setbacks, no past to contend with. Only that which is directly in front of us in that moment.

We choose where to live. In the past, present, future. Only one exists.

Where shall you choose to live?

Chapter 21
There Will Be an End to All of Us

In the light of the tunnel there is an assessment of the risks we have taken and accomplishments to which we have accepted on behalf of Source energy. The dividing of those who stay versus those who remain in the spirit world to watch over depends on the strength of one's willingness to follow their path to destiny.

Destiny is the holy grail for which we seek, the ever-endless place within the spirit world to keep eye on the earthlings below. A feat which most cannot endure because they have lost touch with their inner guiding system and a power amongst their psyche that they do not wish to let go of. Therein lays a key to your destiny. **Letting go completely, wholly, to the divine destiny that is bestowed in you.**

The real issue for us all is seeing and believing that this exists at all. That there can be a spirit world that allows us to take the shackles off, rest in the waters that have held us buoyant if only we could have seen then. That which our eyes cannot see we do not believe, a fault of our belief system and the small vision we have of ourselves as human beings.

When would you have come to see your own power?

When would it have occurred to you that you could have let go rather than resist, thus making yourself lighter and able to navigate the waters of change effortlessly, without pain, without conflict, without hesitation?

The world would be your oyster, gathering power from the waves around you to carry you where you need to go, where you were meant to be all along. Resting when required, tumbling if needed, all knowing that you would be held gracefully to your landing place, amongst friends of all kinds, new and old, the view always changing, always welcoming of you. All of you, as you are, as you evolve from one stage of life to another. You are welcomed and you are home in your final growing place where you can rest and build the most glamorous pearl there could ever be.

Within you you build, and you harness brilliance and beauty. When it is time for your end, you leave for others a mark, a place where you have left visibly an impression of what beauty lies within and without.

We all come to this place at some point, some earlier some later, when we realize what life is all about. And yet we choose still the mundane in the morbid of our worrisome ways. Waking, sleeping, waking, sleeping. The heart has gone to sleep long before, the soul lost even before then. Trying to keep a light on but no one is watching. Not ourselves and not our family or friends, because they are in the same boat. Floating aimlessly, never finding their true north. Looking too far into the distance to notice what is right in front of their nose. Troubled by the past, worried about the future, and never noticing the present—in the presence. **We wake**

to this world eyes wide open yet die when our eyes have been shut for years.

What will it take for our eyes to be open, our ears listening, our hearts in tune with the rhythms that have existed all along?

When will we observe, truly observe ourselves, and the fundamental shift that must take place within ourselves and with society as a whole to allow our brilliance to shine, unfiltered, untethered, unbound?

How this happens at a global scale can only be decided once we individually decide that we can no longer live this way. That there is another way, and we must try. If we do not try, we have lost the opportunity to thrive within ourselves, within our families, and within the generations that lay ahead of us. We have a duty to try a new way, evolve into what we are known that we can be.

Walking across the threshold into the spirit world is like walking the bricks to paradise. Glowing all colors of the rainbow and those that we cannot even imagine. Brilliance. Softness. Clarity. Calmness. Radiance. Allowing all beings to just be. In this place there is no leader. Only guides amongst guides. Each holding wisdom to impart on another. Kindness. Generosity. Amongst friends. Always. There is no alternative. This, is the gift. The destiny that we wish to find but have lost control in the way of knowing. In the way of being.

Where shall we start to turn this ship around. Here, now. Tomorrow and the next.

Choice by choice it is ours to make, one degree at a time, one paddle at a time. It will move. It will take time, but you try and try again until the north star comes perfectly into view.

And then, you have found your way. An ease of being and living. A floating through with a trust that is unwavering. A resilience that is tested by time and tenacity of our own soul's strength and will to be great.

Grand.

Epilogue

T here are heavens upon heavens in which the Universe resides. It's a wonder why we think we are alone. This aloneness kills us, reaps us of all will to choose the highest, the best for our spirit and our well-being. The heavens know that what is possible is within reach for all of us humankind. There is no potential that we cannot reach if we expand our minds and hearts to embrace the power within each of us.

There comes a time when we will each be faced with the question. Is there not more? Is this all there is? At that moment we wake from the slumber of daily living and propel down a new trajectory of inquiry, possibility, and oneness.

There is a life beyond this life, a way which serves each and every one of our higher purposes. The social nature of our humanness requires us to do this together, to serve humanity, and the survival of the earth. We reap what we sow in all manner of the words–in physical, spiritual, and mental planes–we all have the power to build something great.

Our minds and thoughts are not our power, rather they facilitate our work between us as an extension of our soul's desires. Purity of mind is thus essential to allow for the soul's voice to come through, the essence, the truth, and not a conjured story of thoughts and beliefs.

Is this true of my soul?—must be asked when a thought or pattern is taking us elsewhere.

Is this my soul speaking?

The most basic questions we can ask ourselves in times of confusion or chaos.

What does soul want?

There is only one true voice of the soul. All others are ego and the power which we give our thoughts. All others are an amalgamation of energies that do not necessarily serve our highest good.

We learn from that which is untrue until we find the truth within ourselves and each other. **We find our essence through truth, and with essence we can finally expand into our purpose with great ease.** The ever-present truth that we all seek is there for us to see beneath all the stuff that we bring upon ourselves unknowingly, unwittingly.

And with purpose and intent we can unravel all of that which we have built upon falseness. One step at a time.

The End.

Recommended Practices: Book One

Connect to your inner voice and intuition

- Find a space where you can remain in peace and undisturbed quiet for a minimum of 72 hours.

Resolve your fears

- See and hear them, truly and deeply.

- What is causing turmoil within yourself? Pay yourself attention to what requires attention. Regularly. It gnaws because it is important.

- Help other souls remember their light, especially during dark times.

Create and nurture the container for the soul to speak

- Presence, calmness, and a willingness to look inside. BE, fully, and completely, with no demands, no distractions, and no recurring pain. Allow for healing.

- Support efficient functioning of the systems in the lower third of the body (womb, stomach, spleen, and intestines).

- Consume bone broth regularly.

- Breathwork, yoga, and space to be in-body.

- Access your guides and angels regularly.

Shedding and releasing phases

Allow the soul to retract, regenerate, integrate, and alleviate what no longer serves the highest needs.

- Withdraw from daily activities, resume activities when guided and appropriate.

- Lay on a comfortable platform or bed to support stillness.

- Consume pure foods in bright colors to move energy to lighter realms and support digestion.

- Consume warming foods and elixirs to stimulate digestion and heat the body.

- Minimize heavy tasks or activities.

Intention of the whole

- When taking individual action, bring true intention of the whole.

- Individual strength supports the whole. You cannot give from an empty cup.

The weight of the past

- The past is to be learned from not to stay in.

Change beliefs

- Daily, identify where a change in belief needs to occur for the highest good. Bring light to this intention and hold it throughout the day. Walk with it and the place will find you.

Harness kundalini energy

Once per month initially, then once per week maximum, allowing for integration in between. Nurture the soul and physical body during this process, eliminate all toxins and reducing environments. Regularly rest and use relaxation techniques, consume bright foods and beverages, and apply subtle acupressure on the forehead. Resist the urge to process too deeply. Establish a meditation practice in advance.

1. Bring the body and mind to complete stillness and non-thought.

2. Imagine a cord connecting you to the earth's core. Bring earth force into the root chakra and samsidara chakra embedded within. Observe pressure across the pelvic region. Bring this pressure up the main channel across the remaining chakras. When the crown is reached, grasp the skies with your mind's eye, remaining connected with the earth.

3. With upper and lower chakras connected and spinning, envision a powerful light at the base of the spine where it meets the coccygeal region. Use white light to stimulate the region. Maintain safety and presence. Observe the circuit proceed up the spine. Observe visions, feelings, sensations.

Allow what needs to rise and release

- Do not engage the temptations linked to the events. Observe, breathe, and release until it is no longer visible within your mind or body.

- Remain calm and centered to create safety in the nervous system, usurp the fight or flight system to establish a new process that recognizes the sensitivity of the body and deep rooted knowing in the soul.

Ask the basic questions

- Is this my soul speaking?

- Is this true of my soul?

- What does my soul want?

About the Author

Valentina M. Grosvenor, a conscious channeler on a journey of self-discovery and self-actualization, is guided by the spirit world and helps others on their journey home to themselves. Awakening to a new world, life events have paved the way on her spiritual path to unveil her hidden gifts and life purpose. Through willing openness and observation, she holds a deep faith and trust in the wisdom that unfolds, day by day, moment by moment. Like a flower meticulously revealing its delicate, vibrant petals one by one, ever so beautifully and in perfect form with the world around her.